Negotiating

By Louis Zeman

Free membership into the Mastermind Self Development Group!

For a limited time, you can join the Mastermind Self Development Group for free! You will receive videos and articles from top authorities in self development as well as a special group only offers on new books and training programs. There will also be a monthly member only draw that gives you a chance to win any book from your Kindle wish list!

If you sign up through this link http://www.mastermindselfdevelopment.com/specialreport you will also get a special free report on the Wheel of Life. This report will give you a visual look at your current life and then take you through a series of exercises that will help you plan what your perfect life looks like. The workbook does not end there; we then take you through a process to help you plan how to achieve that perfect life. The process is very powerful and has the potential to change your life forever. Join the group now and start to change your life! http://www.mastermindselfdevelopment.com/specialreport

Table of Contents

Introduction

Congratulations on purchasing *Negotiating* and thank you for doing so. The following chapters will provide you with the knowledge you need to become a master negotiator, but it won't happen overnight. Your skill at negotiating is like a muscle, it needs to be exercised regularly. Use the information provided as a guideline when considering the other negotiators, you face and try out tips and tactics that will work according to what feels right.

While initially it may be easy to choose poorly, it will get easier with time. Many negotiators are adept at masking their true intentions, approach each new negotiator with an open mind and try to use each experience to the fullest. At first you will surely miss out on maximizing a few negotiations and it is best to think of those as learning experiences. The path to becoming a master negotiator is a marathon, not a sprint, take your time and you will find the results more than balance out.

Chapter 1: Common Types of Negotiations

While in a perfect world, every negotiation would have a win/win outcome and everyone would walk away happy every time, this is not a perfect world and sometimes there must be a winner as well as a loser. To ensure you are the former more often than the latter, here are the most common types of negotiations that you will likely encounter along with tips to make the best of each situation.

Win/Lose

A win/lose negotiation is the most common type of negotiation that many people will experience. Negotiating the price of car, for example, is win/lose because the car has a fixed value and the purchaser is trying to work to get that price below the set value while the seller is trying to keep the price above that point. The two goals are mutually exclusive and there will be a clear winner and loser in this negotiation.

This is what is referred to in game theory as a zero-sum game. To wit, the pie will never get any bigger or smaller, the players must play the game to determine who gets the biggest slice. When faced with a win/lose negotiation your best course of action is to try and determine the other party's options if the negotiation fails as well as their minimum requirements for satisfaction as keeping the negotiation from reaching those numbers while staying comfortably away from your own minimum numbers is the key to success.

Win/Win

In those rare circumstances where the pie can expand to the point that everyone can have an equal slice, then that is considered a win/win negotiation scenario. Typically, these only occur when both parties are joint partners in a venture as even if one partner does better to start, it is still considered win/win as both parties will ultimately make money on the venture. Salary negotiations can also be considered win/win as can intra-business sales. If the possibility of a win/win negotiation exists, then every effort must be exerted to keep the negotiations as constructive and friendly as possible.

Lose/Lose

The opposite of a win/win scenario, in a lose/lose negotiation everyone is going to get burned and your goal is emerge as lightly singed as possible. Lawsuits are typically considered lose/lose as are any type of negotiation for reparations as the injured party is rarely going to receive compensation greater to the loss and the responsible party has to pay. If you find yourself in a loose/loose negotiation it is important to avoid letting feelings come into play as much as possible. If this happens it is easy for an otherwise beneficial negotiation to turn hostile and aggressive extremely quickly. Strive to keep a collaborative tone and try and determine the other party's minimum requirements for success.

Adversarial

While depending on the circumstances, lose/lose negotiations can at least start out in a civil fashion, adversarial negotiations are always extremely competitive by their very nature. All win/lose negotiations and many lose/lose negotiations end up being categorized in this way. High stakes win/win negotiations can also turn adversarial. In the worst cases both negotiators let their feelings get in the way which can in turn mean they care more about hurting the other party then their own negotiation goals. These sorts of negotiations rarely appear without warning however which means you should have time to plan out an effective strategy for success.

Bad Faith

These types of negotiations occur when at least one party negotiates while at the same time having no intention of sticking to the negotiated agreement after the fact. What's worse, a negotiation can turn to bad faith if one party only suspects the other of wrong doing. These sorts of negotiations are commonly used to delay or deter an undesired series of events or to divert one party's attention from the heart of the issue. If you suspect that the person you are negotiating with is in fact negotiating in bad faith, then your best course of action is to include one or more penalties for failing to keep up the agreement as part of the negotiations.

Collaborative

These types of negotiations are common among business partnership negotiations and other situations that are likely to result in large gains for both parties. These types of negotiations are friendly and non-confrontational and are best handled with a mix of optimism, creativity and persuasion.

Multi-party

These types of negotiations occur between more than two parties and as a result are often quite complicated and can even take months if not years to work through fully. A good example of multi-party negotiations are treaties determining international issues between two or more nations.

Chapter 2: Basics of Negotiation

From buying a house to buying something from a street vendor, being able to negotiate properly is a skill that everyone uses to some extent from time to time. Despite this, it is a skill that few people take the time to truly master. If this sounds like you, here are a few tips to get you started in the right direction.

Two ways to view negotiation

There are two primary views on negotiation which each break the act down differently. The first consists of three primary parts, substance, behavior and process. Substance is considered the actual agenda of the negotiation, the topics that the parties involved are actually negotiating over. Behavior is considered the way the two parties interact with one another, how they communicate and what their relationship is. Finally, process is considered the approach all the parties take when negotiating as well as the greater reasons and issues behind the negotiation.

The other view of negotiation breaks the process down into four separate parts which include: tactics, tools, process and strategy. Tactics comprises all of the most detailed parts of the negotiations including prepared statements and responses to the other party's statements. Tools and process work together and jointly comprise the preparation and follow through of any set steps based on assumptions of the other party. Finally, strategy can be considered the overall goal for the negotiation including acceptable outcomes down through worse-case scenarios.

Know your stuff

Before you enter into a negotiation it is important to always research whatever topic you plan to negotiate, remember, forewarned is forearmed. Likewise, this will help you have a better idea of what you want from the negotiation as well as where to start to ensure you end up where you want to be. Remember, if you aren't clear on what you want, the person you are negotiating with won't know what to give you. Before you enter into any negotiation it is important to have three numbers in mind: your ideal outcome, the worst-case scenario you would agree to in a pinch and the number which would cause you to walk away from the deal entirely. It is important to have all three numbers in your mind at the start of the negotiation so you can gauge how it is going while it is taking place and adjust your strategy accordingly.

Embrace relationships

One key facet of any negotiation is trust, if both sides cannot trust that the other will hold up their end of the agreement then no true negotiation can begin. This is not something that appears overnight however as building a relationship takes time and effort on both sides. If you do not have a lot of time to develop a trusting relationship with the person you are negotiating with then there are a few things you can try to speed through the process.

- Look for common hobbies, interests or background details
- Mind your first impression

- Ensure any promises made can be kept
- Focus on your reliability
- Try humor, if that doesn't work, try flattery
- Avoid looking arrogant or aggressive

Know the alternatives

Before you enter into any negotiation it is important to consider the BATNA (best alternative to negotiated agreement) of all of the parties involved in the negotiation. For yourself this means considering what you will do if the negotiations fall through as well as what the other party is likely to do. Understanding the results for all-sides if the negotiations falter is key if you are to determine just how important the negotiations are to all the parties involved.

Listen

Listen more than you talk. A good negotiator doesn't need to talk incessantly to control the conversation. In fact, listening will often give you insight into what the other person is thinking, sometimes without the person even being aware of what is happening. This can also help you understand the issues the other party is facing and make it easier for the two of you to reach a consensus.

Listen can also be considered an acronym for how you should behave during a negotiation. L stands for looking and acting interested in what the other person has to say. I stands for interacting with the conversation by following up and asking questions. S stands for staying focused on your goals in the negotiation. T stands for telegraphing your understanding of the topic by citing specific facts and figures. E stands for evaluating your message to ensure you are always on point. Finally, N stands for negating your feelings, good negotiators don't let feelings enter into the equation one way or the other.

Other types of communication

When it comes to many negotiations, what isn't said is nearly as important as what is. This is because both your emotions and nonverbal cues routinely affect the other negotiating party. In this case forewarned is forearmed and you can use this information to your advantage without having to resort to any specific negotiation tactics.

Emotion

Despite the fact that their effect on negotiations have really only begun to be studied in recent years, emotions have great power to shape a negotiation for good or ill. While it is important to attempt to separate yourself from your emotions while negotiating, this is a skill that many people have not mastered which means it will inherently play a part in many decisions. Positive emotion are key to coming to reasonable compromises which can ultimately promise great gains while at the same time making it easier to measure out concessions. On the other hand, negative emotions can lead to competitive or hostile feelings and can cause a negotiation to falter all because one of the parties took something the wrong way and let the issue escalate.

Understanding the influence these emotions can have is a powerful tool when negotiating as it can afford you a small measure of control over how the other negotiating party feels. When attempting to influence the way someone you are negotiating with feels, it is important to have enough of a relationship with that person that you can predict their responses to various stimuli. To do this it is important to understand their dispositional affect so you can plan around it accordingly. Dispositional affect comes in two main varieties positive affect and negative affect with either subtly affecting how each of us responds to given situations.

Positive Affect

Those with a positive affect tend to have more confidence and tend to be happier than their counterparts. This will often manifest itself in excessive confidence prior to the start of the negotiations while also making it more likely for them to suggest cooperative strategies. This theme continues throughout the negotiation process and these people will in turn be more agreeable overall and use fewer aggressive tactics throughout the encounter. When compared with negotiators who have a negative affect, those with a positive affect are known to successfully navigate more negotiations while also being less likely to negotiate in bad faith.

This comes about as those with a positive affect tend to show a pattern of better decision making processes including understanding other perspectives, problem solving, thinking "outside the box" and a greater willingness to take risk. In addition, after the negotiation process has been completed, those with a positive aspect will tend to find themselves more satisfied overall when thinking about the outcome and about the future as it relates to that outcome. It is not all good however, as those with a positive affect are habitually unable to judge their own work in an unbiased manner, instead consistently rating themselves above their actual level of performance.

Negative Affect

A negative affect has proven time and again to negatively influence the entire negotiation process, though none so much as anger. When people negotiate angry they frequently resort to more antagonistic strategies and are much less like to cooperate even if the joint solution is relatively win/win. A negative affect will sour a relationship and easily alter a person's primary goal to one that only involves beating the other side. You can use this to your advantage however as negative affect negotiators are more prone to ignoring the other party's arguments or interests which may make It easier to sneak in an extra concession or two.

Choosing the right way to talk to someone with a negative affect can make a huge difference in the outcome. They are much more likely to make self-centered decisions without necessarily thinking through the consequences so if you phrase an offer in a way that appeals to this trait then it is more likely to be accepted. Those with a negative affect are also more likely to make mistakes in general and make suggestions that reduce joint gains.

A negative affect is not all bad however as a genuine show of emotion can be a powerful determining factor in a negotiation if it is timed properly and used sparingly. In addition, it can make for a better negotiation experience in some situations including lose/lose and adversarial negotiations.

The other party's emotions
While your own emotions inevitably play a part in your decision making process, it is important to remember that the other party's emotions will also have an effect on you as well. The other emotions at the negotiation table subtly signal to you what the other person is thinking if only you take the time to look for them. If the person seems to have a positive affect it is important to keep them that way while if they have a negative affect it is important to break their current mental cycle and replace it with something more beneficial.

Besides providing clues to their owner's mental state, the other negotiating party's emotions can also affect you physically. Some emotions such as sadness and disappointment can easily lead to an automatic compassionate response in those with a positive affect which can then in turn lead to extra concessions on behalf of the sympathizing party. The following is a list of what you can expect to happen if you display a certain emotion during a negotiation.

- *Anger:* Displaying anger is most likely to induce a desire to appease by those who are not already adversarial. Depending on the other party it will either promote a desire to dominate or yield.
- *Pride:* Displaying pride is likely to cause the other negotiating party to alter their current strategy.
- *Regret/Guilt:* Displaying either of these emotions is likely to cause the other negotiating party to view you more favorably while at the same time asking for greater concessions.
- *Anxiety:* Displaying anxiety is most likely to cause the other negotiating party to view you less favorably while at the same time expecting somewhat fewer concessions.

Communicating without speaking
It goes without saying that verbal communication is the most important element of any negotiation. What is more surmising however, is just how great of role nonverbal communication also plays in the process. When dealing with another negotiating party it is important to pay attention to how they present themselves as well as their subconscious gestures and body language. Only by taking in everything that the other party is telling you will you be able to get the most out of any negotiation.

Anchoring
A common negotiation tactic is called anchoring, according to this tactic the first party to express their position gains power in the negotiation by determining the starting parameters. The same can also be said of nonverbal cues, and body language anchoring can be extremely effective when used properly. Here are a few forms of body language anchoring you can try during your next negotiation.

- Sitting at the head of the table gives you subconscious authority of the room. Alternately, if you can't claim the seat of power, placing allies on both sides of the other negotiating party can mitigate the head of the table's control.

- Making a positive first impression can go a long way towards forming a beneficial relationship in a short period of time. As such it is always important to greet the other negotiating party with a smile and a firm handshake. Likewise, it is very important to always maintain eye contact to ensure the other negotiating parties feels as though you have nothing to hide.

Deciphering the other party's non-verbal communication
In order to be a successful negotiator you need to be able to understand the other party's nonverbal cues, the ways they interact with the things that person is saying and what it means when the two are at odds. Here are a few examples of nonverbal cues and how to interpret them.

- *Laughter:* When a person laughs at an inopportune time it tends to be either a sign of discomfort or nervousness. In response you should do you best to discover the issue behind the laugh while not specifically linking your curiosity to the laugh.
- *Negative behavior and positive speech:* If the other party seems closed off while talking, drawn in on themselves or refuses to make eye contact, there is a good chance something is bothering them regardless of how positive their words might sound.
- *Clenched fists:* This is a classic example of frustration, regardless of what the other party might be saying. Clenched fists are a sign of barely controlled frustration.

How to tell if you are winning the other party over
While a good negotiator will never tell the other party what they think of them directly, each person has a number of subconscious tells which can show how they feel about a current topic.

- If the other party is receptive to what you are saying they will tend to make eye contact and smile in your direction. Likewise, an unreceptive party may clench their jaw muscles, squint or turn their head away from you.
- Receptive parties tend to sit with their arms spread with their hands relaxed in front of them or on the table. Likewise, unreceptive parties will sit with their arms crossed or with their hands in front of their mouth. Another unreceptive sign is rubbing the back of the neck.
- Receptive parties tend to sit with their legs either spread or together and when standing they ensure they spread their weight across both feet. They also tend to face towards you. Unreceptive parties on the other hand are likely to cross their legs or stand with their weight leaning on the leg which is father away from you.
- Receptive parties tend to lean forward while sitting on the edge of their chairs and make themselves comfortable in the space. Unreceptive parties tend to sit rigidly with their backs to the chair.

Things to remember

- *Start with an honest amount*. While many people find it hard to ask for an amount they really want, this severely limits their success as they force themselves to start out at a disadvantage. The only way the person you are negotiating with will give you what you want is if you ask for it. Start by asking for what you want (or more) and you will be surprised how often the other person will give it to you.

- *Concessions should come from both sides.* Another important part of preparing for any negotiation is determining beforehand what concessions you are willing to make in order to strike a deal. While a good negotiator can always get what they want, they also know that you can't have everything which is why they prioritize aspects of the negotiation to know where to give and where to take. It is also important to know when you are conceding too much and when to concede more.
- *Strive for fairness.* While a good negotiator knows how to get the most out of every deal it is important to ensure that you aren't taking too much without giving back in return. The most productive deals are the ones where neither party feels cheated as it will make any future negotiations with that party much more agreeable.
- *Always get agreements in writing.* Regardless of the agreement struck, it is always important to follow-up the negotiations with an email confirming what was discussed. While some people might find this rude the reality is quite the opposite. Putting the agreement in writing allows both parties perfect clarity on the conversation and prevents any misunderstandings in the future.

Things to Avoid

- *Never be your own worst enemy.* If the person you are negotiating with refuses an offer you make it is important to not immediately come back at them with a lower number. This is what is known as negotiating against yourself and makes you look as though you do not have a list of firm numbers in mind. If you make an offer and it is rejected, wait for the other party to make a counter-offer. If they don't present one immediately, ask what they think would be fair.
- *Never be pressured into making a deal "right now".* If the person you are negotiating with seems extremely keen on getting things finished ASAP, there is a good chance they are trying to force something through that you may not like after closer inspection. Never be afraid to take the time you need to make a good decision.
- *Never negotiate with someone who can't make the decisions.* If the person you are negotiating with takes your offer and says they have to check with someone higher up the chain of command, offer to do that yourself. This is a common negotiating trick and one that you can easily put a stop to by simply asking to speak with the person who makes decisions.
- *Never move forward if your gut says something is wrong.* If something about the deal the other party is offering seems wrong but you can't put your finger on just what it is, hold off. It is important to trust your instincts and look for red flags.
- *Never navel-gaze.* If once a deal has been struck you realize you could have made a better deal it is important to not focus on it. Learning from your mistakes and move on, lingering on them will only cause you to question future deals as well.
- *Never get distracted by ancillary promises.* Often the other party will try and throw in something shiny in an attempt to distract you from what really matters. In general, if the

other party tells you what a good deal or great promotional item something is, the best thing to do is ignore it.

- *Never be afraid to walk away.* If a negotiation is creeping dangerously close to the number at which you walk away, walk away. Don't be afraid to signal your displeasure with the way the negotiations are heading by walking away, remember the deal is bad anyway.

Chapter 3: Effective Negotiation Strategies

Before you start trying out different negotiating strategies it is important to fist determine what type of negotiator you really are. As part of the Harvard Negotiation Project, researchers uncovered that there are three types of negotiators including soft, hard and principled. Learning about your common negotiator type will in turn help you learn what type of negotiating tactics you are likely to be the most effective with while at the same time helping you know what tactics to use to counter the other party's common negotiation strategies.

- **Soft Negotiators:** These negotiators feel that negotiation is akin to competition and just want everyone to get along. As a result, their style of negotiation is gentle, and relies heavily on persuasion and the use of positive relationships to try and get the most out of a bargain. They always try and leave a negotiation on good terms with the other party and strive to always find agreement in every situation. They see the person as part of the negotiation and avoid contests of wills, instead offering solutions and trusting others to stick to their agreements.
- **Hard Negotiators:** These negotiators have no problem using harsh, all or nothing strategies when it comes to influencing the other party. If your response to someone telling you that they don't like your offer is to tell them to take it or leave it, then you are most likely a hard negotiator. These negotiators see each negotiation as a battle and the other party as the enemy. For these negotiators there can only be one winner and they will do what is necessary to ensure that they are it. They see the negotiation as a problem to be solved and count the other negotiating party as part of that problem.
- **Principled Negotiators:** These negotiators focus on the bottom line to the exclusion of commitment to one side or another. They tend to focus on the task at hand and not factor in the personal side of an issue. A principled negotiator will consider a negotiation successful if the goal of the negotiation was met based on objective reasoning, regardless of which side ultimately benefited the most. Objective criteria include things like principles of fairness, moral or professional standards, tradition and other similar ideas.

Outside of these three common archetypes, people can further be broken down by their general disposition as it relates to negotiations. While some people will have a disposition akin to their general negotiation style, others can display differing characteristics depending on how coerced they feel by the negotiations. This is another case where relationship comes into play as it can be difficult to categorize some people without seeing them in action.

- *Accommodation:* Those who are accommodating to others ae often fond of solving other people's problems. They are frequently perceptive of emotional states and can be expected to take the relationship they have to the other negotiating party into account when it comes to determining the best course of action.
- *Avoidance:* Those who are prone to only negotiating when they feel as though they are forced to can be seen as being prone to avoiding. When they do negotiate they tend to

fair rather well as their non-confrontational outlook makes it difficult to pin any agreement down.

- *Collaborative:* Negotiators who enjoy finding joint solutions to problems and almost all principled negotiators can be said to be collaborative. Collaborative negotiators can cause problems when it comes to making unilateral decisions as asking for too much input can turn a simple problem into a complex one.
- *Compromising:* Negotiators who are fond of quickly bringing an end to all negotiations through broad concessions on both sides can be said to be compromising. While being fair is generally important to these types of negotiators, their eagerness for a quick deal can lead them to making too many concessions in short order.

Core Negotiating Tactics

While there are a wide variety of negotiation tactics that are specific to certain types of negotiations, there are a few common practices that useful in almost any situation. While some of these may seem difficult at first, with some practice you will be surprised at how effective they can be.

Brinksmanship

This tactic can be risky unless you know the other party's BANTA and know that they have little choice but to reach some type of agreement. When attempting this tactic, it is important to push a middling agenda that leans in your favor so brusquely that the other party can only walk away or accept. When done properly it convinces the other party to think in a linear fashion about the proposed terms. The most effective counter to a brinksmanship tactic is to simply walk away, regardless of your BANTA, this will show the other party that they must restrain themselves if you are to move forward with any negotiations.

The bad cop and the good cop

This negotiation tactic is taken from the interrogation method of the same name; the only difference is that as long as you have convinced the other negotiating party that you can't make decision on your own you can pull this off all by yourself. To do so you simply start by listing off a number of extremely stringent specifications before apologizing for them, blaming them on someone the other party will never meet, and offering your ideal terms in a new context which makes them seem much more reasonable. Being aware of this tactic makes it easy to spot, though if the bad cop isn't present it can be difficult to verify.

Never commit first

Undervaluing their own position is a common mistake that many people make when entering into a negotiation. While purging yourself of this urge is crucial to your long term success at negotiating, it is also important to remember that the other party in the negotiation is likely struggling with the same issue. As such, if you can get the other party to put forth the first offer you will generally find yourself in the stronger of the two positions.

In addition to the fact that their first offer will frequently be better than what you yourself would have put forth, it also provides you with a general outline of their position while giving them nothing to work with in return. As such, it is then much easier to counter with a number that still meets your needs while at the same time allowing you to set the bracket for further bargaining firmly in the territory you prefer. Ensuring the other party goes first can sometimes be worth millions, just ask Brian Epstein, the Beatle's Manager. In 1963 the band's star was on the rise and United Artists Studio was anxious to cash in on burgeoning Beatlemania.

However, at the same time the studio was unsure if the band was going to go on to be the most famous band of all time or fizzle out before the film came out so they decided to put the movie out for as cheaply as possible. This meant that the band would not be receiving much of a money up front but the studio planned to offer the band as much as 25 percent of the profits from the film so if they stayed popular everyone would win. Armed with these numbers the producer headed off to negotiate with Epstein but he was smart enough to first offer $25,000 and then ask the Beatle's manager what the band wanted without first laying his cards on the table. As such, when Epstein started with an offer of 7.5 percent of the film's profits, United Artist was able to make a killing on *A Hard Day's Night* released in 1964.

Bogey
If during a negotiation the other party suddenly begins to make a large fuss over what by your estimation seems to be a relatively minor point; then there is a good chance they are deploying a bogey tactic in an attempt to trade that small point for a meaningful concession later on. If you believe you are the victim of a bogey, try and bring in a bogey of your own and note the results.

Highball/lowball
Similar to brinksmanship, negotiators fond of this tactic tend to start with either an extremely low or extremely high offer with the goal of making their second offer seem much more reasonable by comparison. It will also allow for additional concessions made on the part of the other party. This can be countered with a layered tactic, sending the unreasonable offer away makes it seem as though it is out of your hands while at the same time not allowing them to use it as an advantage later because you aren't the one who denied them.

Play the fool
Good negotiators have learned that the less the other party thinks you know the more you can get out of them. In fact, as long as you don't lose credibility doing so, there is no end to the positive correlation between apparent relative stupidity and negotiation dominance. The cause of this is two-fold, first the other party will underestimate you and as a result lower their guard; second, it is human nature to help those who are mentally below average rather than using them for selfish ends. While this isn't true of everyone, of course, it is true of enough people to make it a statistically relevant way to diffuse those who seem overly competitive during a negotiation.

To understand why this works so well consider this, think of how difficult it would be to retain a competitive edge when the person you are negotiating with is asking your opinion on the best way to negotiate with you. How would you carry out a plan against someone who responds to specific questions, not with facts and figures you can debate but rather with a simple shrug, a self-deprecating laugh and a return question "what do you think".

Likewise, if you present yourself as a competent and prepared negotiator then you almost guarantee that the other party will work their hardest to counter you. Make things easier on yourself by ensuring you never appear to be any of the following, except of course when it would hurt your credibility to the point of turning the negotiations against you (like during a salary negotiation).

- The sort of person who always knows what they want without taking the time to debate internally and think things over.
- The sort of person who can unilaterally make decisions without "running it by" anyone else.
- The sort of person who is an expert in whatever field the negotiation relates to
- The sort of person who would never concede a major point
- The sort of person whose decision is always final
- The sort of person who never needs to make notes

Playing the part of the fool allows you to retain a wide variety options which will help you maintain the advantage during negotiations. These include being able to believably request additional time to check your notes, consider or research an offer, run the decision by a board or committee or consult legal counsel. You will also be able to more easily plead for more concessions or put other pressure on the other party while still maintaining a positive relationship.

For example, if a hard negotiator comes at you saying that the deal you have proffered has a number of ambiguities, you can throw them off guard by pretending to mull over the word before sheepishly explaining that you know it sounds familiar but it's just not clicking and asking them to explain it to you. This will force them to abruptly change thoughts and possibly gloss over their issue when it comes back around. Even if they don't drop the issue completely, they will then be more likely to approach the topic without their previous vigor. Likewise, it can be used to reinvestigate a portion of the negotiation that you aren't comfortable with while not seeming aggressive yourself. Claiming you don't "quite get" something is much nicer than claiming that you think the other party is wrong and needs to reinvestigate their point.

This tactic is perhaps most effective during win/win negotiations though it will work anytime you feel the need to prevent someone from being overly competitive. Remember, never play dumb in an area that will hurt your credibility with the current negotiations but otherwise don't be afraid to try it out.

Chicken

If you find yourself suddenly blindsided by a number of unreasonable demands in response to a relatively safe offer, then there is a good chance the other party is deploying a tactic commonly known as chicken. Again, this is a tactic that can be negated by knowing the BANTA but otherwise it can be difficult to know if the other party is bluffing. When trying to bluff the other party it is important to either be able to go through with your extreme measures of have a way of backing out of them gracefully in mind before you start.

Snow job

If you feel as though the other party is constantly throwing new numbers and statistics at you then you might be a victim of the snow job tactic. If you find yourself having a hard time telling which facts are relevant, cry off and take the time you need to ensure you make the best decision. If they follow up with an artificial deadline claim the need for expert council.

Think of it as haggling

One common type of negotiation tactic that you will frequently come up against is what many people consider to be "hard-bargaining". These people will approach every negotiation from as firm of a stance in their favor as possible under the assumption that the total amount of the negotiation is fixed so they need to take as large of a share as possible. They will them use any means necessary to ensure they concede as few points as possible throughout the negotiations. The easiest way to counter these types of people is by building a relationship or if that seems to be an untenable solution then adopting your own firm stance and throwing their tactics back at them. While this is a less than optimal solution it is the only way to counter their otherwise immoveable stance. Once they start to give in a little, respond in kind, this may allow for a more beneficial dialogue moving forward.

Layer-up

As previously discussed it is important to never be seen as a person who can make unilateral positions as you can then use each additional person you can imagine a need to gather input from as a reason for a concession or set of concessions. Insulating these layers from one another is crucial as it removes the power to compromise from your purview and can allow you to trade several concessions for the promise that the rest of the negotiated agreement will be accepted.

Nibble

A nibble can be considered any seemingly small concession right before the deal is closed despite the fact that the topic was not raised beforehand. This can be a great way to get a few extra concessions from the other negotiating party though it is easily countered with a firm application of the layering tactic.

Break amounts down to the ridiculous

When a salesperson takes the cost of an item and amortizes it to the point that they can say something like, "for just 50 cents a day" that is considered breaking an item's cost down to the ridiculous. During negotiations it can be beneficial to break costs for the other party down to the ridiculous to make them seem minor enough to not bother over. Likewise, it is important to understand the full cost of any item the other party feels the need to break down in this way as it should be a red flag that they are trying to get away with something. Thus it is important to try and couch your funny money estimates in ways that will not attract notice while being ever-vigilant against those who would do the same to you. Here are a few tricks to keep an eye out for:

- Interest rate which are written as anything other than a concrete figure in currency
- Lots of talk about the monthly cost of a thing without reference to a total amount
- Cost broken down by item or by foot without mention of a total amount
- Increase broken down as hourly instead of as a total amount

Casinos know that forcing people to trade in their real money for chips makes it easier for them to spend more without thinking about the consequences and breaking costs down to the ridiculous works on the same part of the mind. Keep this in mind when negotiating and remember to always discuss costs to the other party in ridiculous terms while at the same time always considering the real world cost of your end of the bargain.

Focus on Deadlines
If you find yourself in a situation where you ultimately have the power in a negotiation, then it can be beneficial for you to set a deadline either to receive an offer or respond to an offer. Setting a deadline is a great response to a negotiator who always seems to need more time or to run the proposal through some new layer of management. It is best to have a favorable BANTA when attempting this tactic however as it can backfire if you overestimate your position.

Place your focus where it will do the most good
Good negotiators know enough to not let the way that the other party acts distract them from their primary goal for the negotiation whatever it may be. Regardless of how the other person acts it is important to always try and separate the negotiation itself from both you and the other party. While it is important to not damage relationships whenever possible, it is equally important to not let the other party's actions influence your perception of the results. Remember, there are plenty of negotiation tactics that involve using the fact that you look angry to your advantage. Never outright dismiss any idea or tactic that will not completely bring the negotiations to a halt.

The flipside of this is that is perfectly acceptable to sometimes appear upset during negotiations as long as the actuality finds you completely in control of the situation. If you let your emotions get the better of you, a safe bet is that is exactly what the other party wanted which means you have already lost the negotiation. If you find yourself having trouble keeping your cool remember to focus on the issues. Instead of letting the other party provoke you take the time to look back through the current negotiations and see how far you have already come.

React Visibly

Taking the time to inhale sharply or make a believable shocked face when being confronted with an offer you don't like can often make the other party question the validity of their offer. This is much more effective than simply verbally indicating your shock or your displeasure. Making this reaction seem natural is key however as a subconscious reaction can be seen as a signal to lower their expectations.

Auction

If you find yourself in a multi-party negotiation with more than one other party biding for the goods or services you provide you can easily use this to your advantage and play the other parties off of one another. If the other parties sense that they might be about to lose out on something this will make them want it even more, increasing your position even further.

Always part amiably

At the end of any negotiation, regardless of whether you win or lose it is always important to offer congratulations to the other party. If you have won the negotiations then this will help to make the other party feel as though they got a better deal compared to what they actually agreed to. If you have lost the negotiation however this will help maintain your relationship with the other party while at the same time planting a seed of doubt that maybe they did not win out as much as it first appears. Even if you do not feel the need to congratulate the other party it is important to never end a negotiation by gloating. You never know when you might have to negotiate with that person again and there is no reason for gloating which is worth having to face an uphill battle in a later negotiation.

Chapter 4: Tips for Negotiating a Job Offer

Regardless if you are interviewing for a position with a new company or a new position in your current company you only have one opportunity to help decide on your starting salary. The following tips will help you come out the other side with most money possible.

Think before you speak
The only time to discuss salary specifics with your employer (or potential employer) is when they have already made you an offer. Despite this fact, a common negotiation tactic for employers is to ask about salary amounts before any offer has been made as if it is just casual conversation. While decades of schooling have trained most people to answer questions correctly and truthfully when asked, in this case nothing could be more incorrect. This can backfire in two common ways, first you ask for too much money and you lose out on the opportunity by making a bad guess; second, you accidentally lowball yourself and leave money the employer was planning on giving you in their pocket instead.

To avoid this trap, ensure you never say anything concrete in regards to salary until you know that you are at least on the shortlist to get the job. If the topic comes up beforehand deflect it by saying you aren't quite sure what all the job entails yet and you don't want to speak out of turn. This can then be followed up by asking specific questions about the job to direct the conversation away from the hot button issue. If instead the other party asks about your current salary then you can disclose it, but remember, when it comes to actual salary negotiations you can talk about what the fair market value for someone with your skills in your region.

Never agree to the first offer
With few exceptions, salary negotiations will never start out at the most the employer is willing to spend. Keep this in mind and never immediately agree to the first offer that is placed on the table. This first rebuttable should be subtle however, start by starring at the suggest amount as if you are really considering it. You don't even need to say anything, instead make a noise in your throat as if you are thinking hard about it. Let this go on for 30 seconds or so and you will frequently hear a better offer soon after.

An important part of this tactic is knowing how much you are actually worth. As discussed above, it is helpful to know what someone with your skillset is worth right now in your area. Use this number to measure when your thoughtful considerations can start to actually become thoughtful. The closer to your current value the number is the less likely pretending to consider it will work. It is also important to use this trick sparingly as it loses effectiveness with each repetition.

Always consider the perks

Before you head into any job offer negotiation it is important to be well-versed in the benefits and perks that the company offers. Depending on how you use them what may seem like a small concession to the employer can add up significantly in your favor over time. Do your homework and it may pay off in the long run. Likewise, if you believe that you are brining something special to the table (and have reasonable data to back it up) it can be worth asking for new benefits as well. As long as you do not go overboard the worse thing the other party can do is say no.

Chapter 5: Tips for Negotiating Sales

When in the business of selling things, it is important to remember to always try and sell the customer first, and negotiate only if it is the only way to keep them from walking away. Not only will this tend to make you more money, it allows you to begin the negotiation knowing more about the customer, thus making the negotiations more effective for everyone.

Know your limits
While you are in the final moments of closing a sale giving the other party an extra 10 percent off might not seem like much of a concession…until you think about it later and realize how much than 10 percent eats into your commission. Having a firm idea of just how much you can do to appease the other party, before you enter into the negotiations, is crucial to long term success.

Never start the negotiations
You have already presented the other party with your best sales offer, if they want to negotiate more then let them set the terms. Doing otherwise is akin to negotiating against yourself. Always listen before you speak.

Don't estimate
While offering a range of estimates can give you some wiggle room, never offer a top of the range greater than you are willing to provide. If you quote a price reduction at 10 or 12 percent the other party is only going to hear 12 percent.

Never start in the middle
If the other party starts a negotiation by asking for half-off, a novice salesperson might return with an offer of 25 percent off and be happy they split the difference. In reality however, studies show that very few people ever expect that much of a discount. Instead of countering in the middle it is important to stay within sight of your original offer. This will imply that you are already near the lowest possible price and that the margin for variance is relatively small.

Only negotiate once
If the other party you are dealing with asks to negotiate the final price, before you do so it is important to ensure that they have the authority to close the deal without having to run any decisions up the chain of command. This is crucial for your bottom line as if you end up having to negotiate with a second party they will often want to start at the point you reached with the first party and work from there. Likewise, it is important to always way until the end of the negotiations to put anything in writing, doing so sooner will only lead to headaches later.

Chapter 6: Tips for Negotiating When Not Face to Face

Despite what many people think, negotiating with someone when you are not in the same room with them has different rules you should follow in order to ensure the negotiation ends in your favor. First and foremost, however, you should keep in mind the fact that the person who initiates contact starts from a higher perceived level of power because they are forcing the other person to put what they are doing aside and focus on the negotiation, right now. Use this to your advantage and always initiate contact whenever possible. With that in mind, consider the following additional tips the next time you find yourself negotiating over the phone or via email.

Another interesting fact which bears consideration when there are multiple negotiation avenues available is the fact that studies show that face to face negotiations tend to favor the negotiating party with the most real world power. The results are reversed in virtual negotiation scenarios, however, as when people are no longer face to face their subconscious responses to authority figures do not activate, allowing them to negotiate with a clearer mind, and leading to better results 100 percent of the time. What's more, this effect can be seen regardless of the number of people who are involved or what the specifics of the negotiations may entail.

This interesting fact of human biology can be used to your advantage in any type of negotiation scenario. It is important to keep it in mind and to use either face to face or video conferencing negotiation avenues when you are negotiating from a position of power and avoid them whenever possible if you are instead negotiating from a weaker position. Remember this fact and use it when strategizing and you will find you always have the proper mindset for the negotiation at hand.

Phone negotiations
Have a plan of action
When preparing to make a phone call that is likely to result in negotiations, it is important to never pick up the phone until you have a clear plan in your mind as to how you want the conversation to go. Only planning as far ahead as the small talk will open you up to potential conversation derailment or other distractions to creep in and prevent you from reaching your goal. Plan out your primary goals for the conversation as well as the talking points you will need to cover to attain each. While you don't need to go to the trouble of writing out everything you will say during the conversation, you will be surprised at just how effective seeing the outline in front of you during the conversation will be.

If the phone call you are making is part of a series, make sure to start each call with a recap of where things ended in the previous call using as positive a spin of the preceding events as possible. Likewise, at the end of each call, make sure you recap what ground has been covered during the call that is concluding and outline what you would like to discuss the next time a phone call is initiated. It is important to always discuss what is coming up next as nothing will damper future phone call based negotiations more than a sense that despite multiple discussions, the topic in question is essentially treading water.

Don't be afraid to do research, either prior to the first conversation or between negotiation sessions, forewarned is forearmed and having access to a wide variety real world scenarios that relate to the negotiation topics will only help your case. What's more, showing that you are extremely well-versed on the topic in question is likely to impress the other negotiator. While this will be unlikely change their position all on its own, the knowledge that you understand all sides of the issue will prevent the other person from try to blindside you with questionable facts and make the negotiation as a whole more effective.

Ensure you remain active during the conversation
When you first make contact with the other party, it is important not to jump right to business and take the time to engage in appropriate small talk. Your ultimate goal is to be as engaging as personal as possible, remember, the only connection the other person has to you is your voice. This means you are missing out on important body language opportunities that need to be filled in somewhere, take cues from the other person as far as appropriate small talk and take pains to remain as affable as possible, even going so far as to make jokes when appropriate. This will be the only chance you have to build a rapport with the other person, don't squander it.

Without physically occupying the same space as the person you are negotiating with; It can be difficult to indicate that you are engaged in what the other person is saying if you do not take the time to take notes and ask questions appropriately. You need to ensure that the other party remains as interested in the conversation as possible in order to achieve the desired results and to make it easier to win them over to your way of thinking.

Taking notes will also make it easier to make sure you are aware the instant that miscommunications arise. By not being in the same room with the other party you are missing out on potential body language cues that can clear up a variety of miscommunications on the spot; double check any potential blind spots as quickly as possible to ensure that everyone remains on the same page. Nothing will derail a potentially positive negotiation faster than a small miscommunication left unchecked until it escalates exponentially, do yourself a favor and make sure everything is as clearly spelled out as possible.

This means it is also important to give the call you are making your upmost attention. Turn off any other screens you may be looking at and focus completely on engaging in the conversation and taking notes as appropriate. Multitasking is a myth, the only thing you are doing when multitasking is working on two tasks in disjointed chunks. What's more, if you are fully engaged in the negotiations and the other person is multitasking you'll have an even greater chance of walking away with a more favorable outcome. Every negotiation is important, make the extra effort to treat them as such.

Always Follow Up

When you are in a face to face negotiation you are virtually guaranteed to have the other party's complete attention. When it comes to phone negotiations, however, the time between the point your conversation ends and the time the other person acts on the information you gave them could be substantial. This is why it is important to follow up phone negotiations with an email that verifies the details so that everyone remains on the same page. This will allow you to follow up with potential future clients in a way that will be easy to refer to in the future and to ensure that they retain your contact information while at the same time not containing the same stigma that calling to reconfirm details holds. It also allows you to remain in the other party's consciousness for a prolonged period, allowing them the extra time they may need to come around to your way of thinking.

Email Negotiations

The limitations of email when it comes to negotiations are similar in magnitude to the differences in face-to-face interactions versus those made using a telephone. When talking to the other party during a negotiation you lose out on the ability to use body language, when emailing in regards to a negotiation, you lose out on the ability to judge the other party's tone as well. This can make it difficult to judge the efficacy of attempted negotiation techniques but it also means that a simple, quality argument that is well-stated can be more effective in this medium than in any of the others. Words have the potential to be extremely powerful as they operate in more of a vacuum than other negotiation avenues, don't take this effect lightly.

Take the time to layer in some extra personality into your responses as a way to humanize yourself without going overboard when it comes to sharing personal details. Consider the following examples:

- Show that you are a real person with a life outside of the negotiation by starting you email by apologizing for the delay in your reply because you were out of the office for a medical issue, spending time with family, or something similar. Talk about how happy you are to be back at work now that things are returning to normal, though you are really swamped because of it.

- Express concern for the other party's wellbeing because of something recent that occurred such as when they took over their current position of when the person you worked with previously left the company. Express empathy, explain that you don't want to add more work to the pile, then couch the issue that needs negotiating in the most reasonable terms possible.

- Take the time to genuinely express some emotion that is typically lacking in buttoned up corporate emails. Explain how the lack of forward progress that is currently taking place has you frustrated at your own inability to push through it before connecting your feelings to those it is likely for the other party to express as well. Use the mutual feelings as a bridge to make positive inroads on the topic that you want to see resolved.

- Take the time to prepare beforehand so you can include as many questions and requests for data as possible. Giving the other party a concrete path forward will allow them to commit to the project more fully sooner than might otherwise be the case and thus be more committed overall when it comes to finding a solution no matter what. In these situations, it is important to ensure that you express your desire and confidence that a mutually beneficial solution can be reached.

When in doubt use video conferencing

While the tips above will allow you to make the most of what are otherwise less than ideal negotiation situations, the best way to ensure that you have as many of the advantages of seeing the other person as possible, is to see as much of the person as possible. These days, the high-quality internet connections and vast array of devices which also contain front and rear facing cameras means that it is easier than ever before to simply set up a video chat and see the other party's face at the very least.

Video conferencing offers a number of advantages over email negotiations, including real time reactions from the other party, but is also superior to a simple phone call as the additional information conveyed by facial expressions cannot be understated. Consider the following tips when it comes to making the most of video negotiation opportunities.

Ensure the process is as simple as possible

Just as with phone calls or emails, it is important that you initiate video conference contact with the other negotiating party to ensure you enter the negotiation from a position of power. Unlike with the other methods of communications, it is important to ensure that the video conferencing solution you use is as simple for the other person to access as possible. Selecting a confusing or finicky video conferencing solution could needlessly delay the negotiation and force the other person to start from a flustered or annoyed state which will make them inherently less receptive to whatever ideas you are presenting. Before selecting a video conferencing provider, do your homework and choose the one that is right for you.

In addition to choosing a simple to use solution for the video conferencing, it is important to email the other party prior to the scheduled meeting time to ensure they have the ability to participate in video conferencing and that their webcam is fully functioning. This will allow both parties to double check that all equipment is working properly and fix any kinks without delaying the negation itself. If the other party does not have a webcam, consider your strengths and weaknesses when it comes to negotiating and then compare the cost of a webcam to the benefits of having the negotiation go your way. Depending on the results, buying the other party a surprisingly cheap webcam may be a viable option.

Take advantage of the format

Once you have taken the time to ensure that everything is set up to allow for a video negotiation, the biggest mistake you can make is to then treat it the way you would a regular phone call based negotiation. Take the time to make the most of your ability to send and receive facial cues, project your authority when it comes to the matter in question and use hand gestures to convey your over-the-top energy levels. In addition, many video conferencing solutions offer the ability to including multimedia portions such as PowerPoint presentations which can make up for the defect when it is compared to face to face negotiations.

Finally, video negotiations tend to end with more successful results because once you have come to an agreement most video conferencing solutions provide you with the opportunity to send over contract agreements instantaneously so that the other party doesn't have the time to rethink any of the excellent points you made while waiting for an actual contract to appear. Everyone knows that the more excited the other party is, the more likely they are going to stop thinking and start acting, take advantage of this fact and use it to your advantage whenever possible.

Chapter 7: Tips for Getting the Price You Deserve for Your Goods or Services

Be confident

When it comes to sealing the deal, many of those who work in sales remain too eager when it comes time to negotiate the final price. This comes about due to the largely mistaken assumption that if they are not willing to lower their prices they will ultimately miss out on the sale. In fact, the opposite tends to be true and clients respect a salesperson who is able to articulate why their product or service is worth paying a little bit more to obtain. Never worry about being rejected outright for the price you present, very few customers will walk away outright without discussing the specifics. Approaching this discussion in the proper way will allow both parties to walk away happy, but only if you are willing to put in the necessary work.

Next you will need to remind yourself that your price is reasonable and that you deserve to receive it; while this may sound like something that does not bear repeating, in reality it is important to repeat this affirmation like a mantra during the negotiation as it will help you to find the mindset required to make the most of the situation. When it comes to defining reasonable, remember that anything you can convince the customer to pay is a reasonable amount. Don't make the mistake of undervaluing your service, you never know what a customer is willing to pay until you ask them. The more valuable your service is, the wider the range of viable variables will be. Focus on improving overall value and let the reasonable price take care of itself.

Having confidence in your product or service is a crucial step towards getting the price you deserve for your goods or service. Since you won't be dropping your price, you instead need to be able to explain to the customer why the product or service that you are offering is worth what you are trying to sell it for, and having a persuasive, truthful reason as to why that is the case will make the entire process go much more smoothly. Don't hamstring yourself when it comes to pricing, don't just tell customers that your product or service is worth the full price you are suggesting, believe it.

When you present the price you are hoping to get for your goods or service never indicate regret over what you have presented by saying that you are sorry or that you wish there was more you could do regarding the price. This ties back into having confidence, you have no reason to feel sorry about what you are offering, because you know it is not just an acceptable price but actually a great deal at the price you offered. Getting the customer to accept your proffered price is all about framing, you only have so much time to spend with each person, make it count.

Finally, make a habit of always having several potential sales on deck at all times. If you become too committed to any one sale, slashing prices to make it a reality begins to look more and more appealing. Doing so will cause you to present yourself in an uncertain fashion when it comes time to negotiate which will then make it easier for the customer to sense your nervousness. Presenting yourself with confidence has already been discussed, knowing you have other sales on the backburner will make doing so even easier.

Prove the worth of your product or service
After you have firmly outlined the lowest price you are willing to accept when it comes to selling your goods or service the next step will be to present the information that indicates why your goods or service is worth the price you quoted the customer. The first step is to couch your price in legitimacy and the best way to do so is to compare it to the market average, if your price is above the average, determine what extra services or benefits come with your goods or service and determine what those extras would cost when paid for individually. If you cannot ultimately justify your predetermined price, then it might be time to reassess. It is important to use readily available data when making these determinations so that if the customer goes and does their own research they will come up with numbers comparable to those you presented.

You should make a point of never starting a conversation with a customer without a firm price you want to receive for your goods or service in mind. Once you do so, you will them be able to feel out the customers you speak with to assure that everyone is on the same page. If you get the feeling that you and the customer are not on the same page, there is no shame in asking them for the budget they are working with or possibly an acceptable range of prices they are interested in. This will save everyone time in the long run and help to find them a solution that works for them.

Have predefined concessions
Obviously there will always be scenarios where it makes more sense for you to play ball with certain customers, but you should always do so in a way that allows you to save face. For example, if while talking to the customer they indicate that they might have additional business in the future then it would be worthwhile to suggest a reduced rate for multiple sales up front. Regardless of the specifics, it is important that you never offer up a concession that causes the balance of power in the negotiation to slip out of your favor. Don't be afraid to offer an ultimatum, if your goods or service is worth it, the customer will always come around to your way of thinking sooner or later.

While having predefined concessions will help you stick to favorable exchanges on the fly, it is also important to make sure that you never appear too anxious to make these sorts of deals. If you offer up concessions, even those that require bulk purchases, too quickly it will make it seem as though you value your goods or service less than you actually do, a move that will cause the customer to reflect this nonproductive viewpoint. Remember, it is always best to hold out on making concessions as long as possible to artificially enhance their value to the maximum amount possible.

The ultimate goal of providing concessions is to make each customer feel as though they are a unique asset to your business that is appreciated as such. Ultimately, a satisfied customer who pays less today is always worth more than a dissatisfied customer that paid full price. To leave each customer feeling as satisfied as possible it is important to always listen to any complaints they might have. Even if you don't make any changes, as remaining firm is important, they will ultimately appreciate the opportunity you gave them to vent. Make sure you can explain the reasons behind your pricing in detail so you can answer any questions they might have before reiterating the unique strengths of your goods or service and sticking to your guns.

Be ready for common customer responses
While no two customers are truly alike, most people tend to approach negotiations using one of three main tactics. Some people like to response in an initially overly negative way either by raising their voices, choking, or making exaggerated facial or hand movements. The reality is that they are actually not all that surprised by your offer, they are simply looking to see what your response will be. If this happens to you, it is important to stay the course and wait for them to add something productive to the conversation. If they don't say anything more, your best bet is to repeat your offer and reiterate its unique value once again.

An additional tactic that is used quite frequently is when the customer counters your offer with the declaration that they can get the same product or service elsewhere for a cheaper price. The best response to this tactic is also to reiterate what about your goods or service that makes the price not only reasonable, but a bargain. During this part of the negotiation it is important to take the customer's focus off of the price of the product or service and onto how much they actually want what it is that you specifically are selling. Once you can convince them that the price is simply a small speed bump in the process, they will be more willing to defer to what you have already established.

Another common tactic that many people, especially those who appear weak, frail or as though they are already dealing with tragedy often attempt is explain their situation in the most tragic way possible before explaining that they only have X amount to spend on your goods or service and that's that. When confronted with this scenario it is important to remain completely nonplused by what you are hearing, reminding yourself that it could just as easily be a lie as the truth if required.

Showing any response to the information that they present will open you up for further attempts along these lines and will make it much more difficult to have a conversation that is productive to either party. Instead of giving in, call their bluff by asking about their finances and appearing as though you are considering what they tell you and how they can draw from other areas to afford your product. Reemphasizing the value of what you are offering is also a valid strategy.

You are halfway done!

Congratulations on making it to the halfway point of the journey. Many try and give up long before even getting to this point, so you are to be congratulated on this. You have shown that you are serious about getting better every day. I am also serious about improving my life, and helping others get better along the way. To do this I need your feedback. Click on the link below and take a moment to let me know how this book has helped you. If you feel there is something missing or something you would like to see differently, I would love to know about it. I want to ensure that as you and I improve, this book continues to improve as well. Thank you for taking the time to ensure that we are all getting the most from each other.

Chapter 8: Tips for Negotiating with Creditors

While many people think of debt as a fixed amount which is set in stone, the reality is quite the opposite. In fact, many creditors will settle for between 25 and 50 percent of the total amount owed which means it is in your favor to attempt to negotiate over debt whenever possible. With that in mind, it is important to do some homework before attempting to negotiate with creditors.

First and foremost, it is important to understand that negotiating with creditors can take several attempts but nearly all types of unsecured debt can be settled for no more than 50 percent of the original total. If you cannot reach this sort of agreement the first time, do not be afraid to walk away. On the flipside however, understand that the creditor will continue to call, send letters, even threaten legal action until the negotiations are completed. Throughout this process it is important to know how your creditor is likely to act next and to understand if your debt is secured or unsecured.

While it is easier to avoid paying the full sum on unsecured debt, it is important to remember that there are laws in place to limit what attempts to collect on a debt can entail and even how long a debt can be attempted to be collected upon. It is also important to consider the legal costs of bringing a suit against you versus the amount of money you owe. Legal battles are expensive and it will rarely be in their best interests to follow through on a court case, regardless of their threats.

The following suggestions work with any type of creditor or local debtor though the success rate can vary depending on the type of debt owed. Local business people, unsecured loans, credit card companies and loans made from local banks are often easy to modify. Meanwhile, student loans and any loan that came from a major bank is much more difficult to negotiate better terms for.

Always start with bankruptcy
Regardless of how likely a scenario bankruptcy is for you, explaining to the creditor that you have been having a hard time making payments and have been looking into every available option can make them much more receptive to negotiating. As a rule, creditors will get less from a person who has declared bankruptcy, even if they have a legitimate claim to the debt which means their negotiators are told to do whatever is possible to ensure that doesn't happen.

Be ready to make a payment
For creditors, getting some money now is better than nothing indefinitely. This is why it is a good idea to explain that you have the cash on hand now to pay off a percentage of the debt (under 25 percent) and start the negotiations there. Make sure you explain that you have a certain amount of the debt on-hand (and make sure you do) and are ready to make a settlement payment immediately or within a few days.

Chapter 9: Tips for Negotiating Large Purchases

When it comes to negotiating for large purchases such as vehicles there are a number of standard tactics which apply in the search for the best deal.

Regardless of what you are told the price is always negotiable
Most sales people will be looking to break the price of the item down to the ridiculous and will be interested in talking about the monthly payment versus the total cost. Start by asking to negotiate with the person who will have the final say and don't let them discuss anything but the total price of the vehicle, after taxes and fees.

Set fixed terms for the negotiation
Start by determining what amount you are willing to pay for the item by researching average prices in your area. Insist on a price as near your goal as possible and stick with it until the other party gives in. Assuming you did your research and your offer is reasonable there is no reason they should not be able to work with you on reaching an acceptable price and until they do don't let them move the conversation to another topic. If they instead ask about trade-ins, explain you are looking into your options but don't want to discuss it until the price has been finalized. If they instead ask about extras, pass.

Regardless of whether it is true or not, when asked about financing say that you are already approved for a loan and are willing to pay with cash, though you would be interested in hearing about dealer-financing. Only allow this topic of conversation once the final price has been negotiated. If the other party continues to try and negotiate the price, again refer to your starting offer and explain that you are not interested in wasting anyone's time with excessive price negotiations and that you are prepared to leave rather than going back and forth indefinitely. Any further conversation along these lines should be met with a stony silence. If you get transferred to a more senior sales associate it is important to repeat the previous steps verbatim and to continue this process until then know you are serious. Following this pattern will guarantee you are in control of the situation.

Initially the other party will most likely issue a blanket denial, claiming that the dealership will not allow the vehicle to go for such a price. At this point it is helpful to have research you can point to and explain that other dealerships seem willing to meet your demands. If the other party continues to use a layer tactic, ask to speak with someone who has more authority.

Keep your loan short
If you must take out a loan to afford the purchase it is important to keep the terms as short as possible. Vehicles and similar items depreciate every year which means the longer you are paying for the vehicle the less of a return you are getting on your money.

Chapter 10: Tips for Negotiating Prices When Buying a Car

As previously discussed, in face to face negotiations the person with the most power starts at a natural advantage. While the person who is selling a car, especially at a dealership, is generally that powerful person, there are a number of tactics you can employee in order to even the odds, or even, turn them in your favor. When you first begin the search for a new vehicle it is important to visit numerous dealerships while looking at what is available while always keeping a few things in mind to make any potential future negotiations more likely to go in your favor.

When looking at available stock, it is important to let the salesperson know that you are just browsing at the moment and have no intention of buying today. This will frame all future actions in a positive light while also keeping the sales person from pressuring you too thoroughly. Feel free to give out general descriptions of the cars you are interested in but avoid specifics that include price ceilings or questions about trade-in value or monthly payments as those are likely to come up much later in the process. Getting ahead of yourself at this point could lock you into an unfavorable starting negotiation position. Whatever you do, be polite and courteous to the salesperson as you will likely be dealing with them if you do plan on using that particular dealership to find your new car.

Know the right time to submit your ultimatum
First and foremost, you should start every car buying experience by presenting the salesperson with a well-researched and reasonable offer and telling them that they can contact you when they are able to meet it. While this won't always result in immediate success, it will likely work in your favor sooner than later. It is generally a good idea to present your offer to a salesperson around the middle of the month and then follow up two weeks later when the end of the month rolls around. Enough time will have passed to show that you were serious about walking away while also allowing you to check on the vehicle you were interested in without losing face.

Your reappearance at the end of the month also provides them with the opportunity to get one more sale in, a real boon especially if the rest of the month happens to be subpar when compared to their average. This also goes for coming back at the end of the night on a Saturday or days that were terrible for people window shopping thanks to inclement weather or important local events. Getting the best deal from a dealership is simply a matter of picking the best moment that tilts the balance of power in your favor.

Dealing with a private seller
When it comes to buying a vehicle from a private seller there are a few important things that should be assessed in order to determine how much variance you can expect to get out of the price. Many private sellers have external reasons for selling the vehicle that may make them more open negotiation, when finding out additional information about the vehicle it is important to always ask to why the other party is selling the vehicle and see if the story behind it can be used to your advantage. Using the information that you have acquired, you can then make an opening offer on the vehicle that is somewhat lower than the listed price but make up

the additional value by pointing out the fact that you can get the full offered amount in cash that same day. The promise of an easy end to their time with the vehicle is frequently enough to push most people over the edge towards a sale.

Don't be afraid to ask questions
Regardless of who you are buying the vehicle from, you should never be afraid or nervous to ask the seller how flexible they are on the listed price. While on the surface this question doesn't seem very useful, after all, practically everyone selling a vehicle is open to negotiation, at least to a partial degree. In reality, however, the answer to this question and the way it is answered can provide you plenty of valuable negotiation information. In general, the more enthusiastic their response, the more flexible the price is. In addition, they could give out useful information including the floor on the price or additional tidbits that could come in handy later.

If the information you are given in return doesn't make it sound as though you and the seller are going to realistically be able to make a deal, it is important to never give up hope before making a thorough effort to make the most of your situation. Even if your budget is below the stated minimums it will never hurt to explain your maximum and see what happens in response. As long as you do so politely and explain that what you are saying is in an effort to save everyone some time, you will be surprised at how many additional doors it may open. Always tell the seller to give you a call if anything changes; you never know what will happen if you are willing to wait long enough.

Don't get anxious
If a negotiation starts to swing in your direction, especially if things happen much more quickly or more easily than you initially imagined, it can be perfectly natural to get excited and work to close the deal right there on the spot. However, it is important to never get so caught up in the excitement of winning a negotiation that you forget to have any type of used car inspected thoroughly prior to signing any documents. An ounce of prevention is worth a pound of cure, if the vehicle is in good condition then the seller should have no problem waiting for you to have it completely checked out before making a deal.

Negotiate Separately
After the salesperson has agreed to your offer, it is important to remember that if you are not paying cash for the vehicle, you will want to negotiate the amount you are getting for your trade-in (if any) as well as the terms of repayment separately. This will allow you to negotiate each part of the scenario individually so you don't lose out in one area to benefit in the other.

When it comes to negotiating what your trade-in vehicle is worth, it is important to do research beforehand to ensure you know what you are working with. Likewise, if you have made any improvements to the vehicle it is important to be able to point them out and to have a reasonable idea as to what additional value they bring to the vehicle. When it comes to negotiating the terms of your repayment, it is important to remember that lower isn't always better as the interest rate tends to spike with each additional 12 months added to the repayment plan which means the overall amount you will be paying for the vehicle increases significantly. Remember to stay within your means when it comes to picking a new car and avoid the potential headaches of trying to find ways to pay for it later.

Chapter 11: Tips for Negotiating Prices When Buying/Selling a House

There are few things more stressful in life than either buying or selling a home. While the housing market is nowhere near as tumultuous as it once was, that hasn't made the experience easier for anyone involved. Here are a few tactics that you can use no matter what side of the process you are on:

- Remain silent, this is good advice regardless of how you are submitting offers or counter offers. The response to an offer sets the tone for the remainder of the negotiations and if you take the time to simply act self-assured at your price while appearing completely comfortable with the silence then the other party has no choice but to respond. To seal the deal, repeat your current offer after 30 seconds of silence have passed, don't elaborate just repeat the facts. The likely response to this tactic is a concession from the other side, make it count.

- Take advantage of body language, when you are in the same room as the other party, take advantage of that fact by using body language to convey negative emotions without appearing needlessly argumentative. A well placed wince can set the stage for the type of negotiations you want moving forward while forcing the other person to acquiesce to you before the real negotiations have even started.

Regardless of which side of the experience you are on, however, there are negotiation tactics that you can use to ensure that you come out the victor once the dust has settled.

Getting the best deal when buying a home

When it comes to buying a new house, the most important thing to remember is that in order to make a realistic and competitive offer on a particular home you need to be familiar with the local market, including specifics as close to your desired lot as possible. Outside of what other properties in the area have sold for, it is important to understand what the supply versus demand is like in the area in question. For all of these reasons, it is often best to hire a realtor who can help you to more easily understand the unique facts about your potential new home. Beyond that, it is important to enter into any negotiations preapproved for a mortgage so you can have the confidence to negotiate specifics knowing you can follow through. Keep the following in mind once you have found your dream home and are looking to close a deal.

Be flexible

While everyone likes to win when coming out of a negotiation, when it comes to buying a home, it is important to focus on any serious issues that may need addressing instead of squabbling over amounts under $10,000. For example, the difference between a home that is $200,000 and $205,000 is only $21 per month. Take the concessions the other party asks of you seriously and determine their true costs before committing either way. It is important to remember what is truly at stake for these negotiations and not to let the perfect home slip away in an effort to win an ultimately minor point.

Regardless of whether or not the area you are looking in can be considered a "buyer's market," it is important to ask for concessions, including repairs, on the part of the seller. There is no harm in asking as long as you are not overly committed to the changes you requested. It is generally best to wait until you have had the property inspected to make these sorts of requests as you will not have the chance to make them again once the terms have already been made. Prior to entering into negotiations it is important to also determine why the seller is moving and what, if any, concessions that this information may contain. If you know the seller is looking to modify the closing period or has other personal needs that relate to the home, you can better use these to bargain for concessions of your own. Go into the negotiation phase prepared for anything and you'll walk away happier, guaranteed.

Placing the right offer
When it comes time to formally submit an offer, it is important to base it on what the actual value of the home is worth, rather than on the list price. Take into account where the price is in relation to homes in the area and pick your battles, the price for homes listed below market value is unlikely to budge, while those that are listed above value are worth the effort of true negotiation.

Especially when it comes to competitive markets, it is important to ensure your offer is appropriate for the property in question as taking chances on a lowball offer can easily result in that offer being ignored as the seller moves to the next one on the list. Be competitive, not insulting. If you really like a property, there is no shame in asking for an inspection prior to the point where negotiations begin, remember you only get one chance at negotiation, make it count.

Let the negotiation begin
Once you are ready to negotiate on the price of a home, you will need to determine a negotiation strategy based on the information that your research revealed about the area in question. If the area you are looking to purchase property in is a buyer's market, you as the buyer, unsurprisingly, have the power going into the negotiation. This means that properties are likely to take much longer than normal to sell which in turn means that sellers are anxious to do as much as they can to keep potential buyers interested.

The best way to take advantage of this situation is to start by making as many demands as possible in order to concede some of them in exchange for the ones you want the most. A few popular choices include:

- Start with an offer that is approximately 10 percent lower than the amount you ultimately wish to pay for the property.
- Ensure that the seller will pay all of the closing costs on your time table.
- Ask for appliances or large pieces of furniture, lawn furniture etc.

If the market happens to be in the seller's favor, then buyers have much less clout and the wrong type of offer can cause you to lose out on the home you had your eye on. In these scenarios, a reasonable, firm offer that is quickly made tends to be the best course of action. When it comes to contract contingencies, you will only be able to negotiate for things like inspection and appraisal, otherwise the seller holds all of the cards.

If the market that you find yourself in has an appropriate number of houses for sale, then it is important to go into any negotiation expecting it to take longer than in either of the more extreme scenarios as personal priorities on either side are likely to expose themselves leading to multiple counter offers. In these situations, it is important to know what concessions are crucial for the other party to make and what concessions you yourself will never be comfortable making. Your initial offer in this scenario should be below the asking price and include reasonable contingencies as well as a few that swing for the fences to give yourself some room to come to an agreement. More so than other scenarios, neither party is likely to proceed if they don't feel as though they are profiting from the negotiation.

Getting the best deal when selling your home
When it comes to selling your home, you are likely to hear all sorts of crazy offers and plenty of crazy buyers making unreasonable demands for concessions. In addition, it is important to take the time early on to divorce your feelings for the home from the selling process as otherwise it can be difficult to let negative comments slide which can lead to counterproductive exchanges between buyers and sellers. That's why it is important to keep the following tips in mind in order to ensure you walk away from your former home as well off as possible.

Selling can give you leverage in bank mortgage negotiations
If you are behind on your mortgage, the fact that you are now selling your home can give you a significant edge in negotiating with the bank on your past due bills. In these scenarios it is important to seek out the head of the loss mitigation department of your lender and bluntly explain the specifics of your situation. As long as you explain the entirety of the scenario, you will be surprised how willing most lenders are to wait for, or to otherwise reduce, payments. A foreclosed property helps no one, working out a solution in these situations is in everyone's best interest.

Remain vague
Prior to any eventual negotiations, you will want to remain as tight lipped as possible when it comes to explaining to any real estate agents or potential buyers the reasons you decided to move. Events such as moving for a new job, getting a divorce or having difficulty paying the mortgage are all things that can be held over your head in hopes of getting a better price on the property because it is clear that you are in a hurry to sell. Instead, it is important to already have a simple, easy answer when someone inevitably asks you why it is you are selling your home. Blame it on the weather, your spouse's family, or even the strength of the current housing market, whatever your excuse is, stick to it and keep it vague.

Counter aggressively
Assuming you are not in a seller's market, the first offer that you receive from potential buyers will likely be a lowball bid designed to get you to come down from your asking price to start the

negotiation off in their favor. The way that most sellers counter this offer is by coming back with something lower than their list price but higher than the price the buyer offered. This will certainly help move the process of selling the home along, but it will also go a long way towards dropping the total price you can expect to see for the home.

Assuming you took the time to research the current fair market price of your home, countering with your list price shows that you know what you have and that you stand by your initial assessment. While some buyers will ultimately walk away when confronted with this approach, many more will come back with a more reasonable offer that you can then work with more readily. If you don't want to appear inflexible while at the same time retaining as much of the list price as possible, instead concede a nominal amount, something like a thousand dollars, to show that you are not completely inflexible.

Reject the offer flat out
Depending on the offer the buyer submitted, a simple counteroffer at your listing price may not be enough, if this is the case, the right course of action may then be to simply reject their offer outright and invite them to submit something more suitable instead. This sort of response is only really viable when you are certain that your listing price is fair for the quality of the property in question. If the buyer returns with a second offer, even if it is just a few thousand dollars higher, you will enter into the negotiation proper from a greater position of power.

This strategy also keeps you free to play the field in hopes that a more appropriate offer comes along while the initial buyer is deciding whether or not to submit a new offer. The fact that this is the case will also motivate the original potential buyer, assuming they are still interested, they will then want to move quickly to lock down the property or risk losing out completely. This is particularly the case if the property has been listed recently or if a public showing is pending.

Create an arbitrary timeframe
Another way to create a more powerful negotiation position for yourself is to place the house on the market but refuse any offers prior to a date that is typically after an open house. This will plant the idea in potential buyers' minds that there is already competition for the property, even if there really is none. This strategy almost always results in higher initial bids and may even lead to a bidding war if there are multiple interested parties.

The same goes for any counteroffers that you submit once an offer on the property has been made. These are legally binding negotiations and it is important to treat them as such which means it may be in your best interest to put a timeframe on your offer to ensure that you are not put in a position where a better offer comes along that you are unable to consider because you are already in negotiations with a buyer who is taking their sweet time coming back with a counter to the counter offer. The key is setting a deadline that is pressing while at the same time not so short that the buyers don't have time to return another offer. Consider a timeframe that is one day less than the standard limit for such things in your state to show buyers your serious about moving forward with the home selling process.

Make the right concessions

When it comes to negotiating with buyers, agreeing on who is going to be paying the closing costs can be a real sticking point in otherwise productive meetings. These fees can often be difficult for buyers, already strapped for cash from the process of buying and moving into a new home, to attain in a reasonable period of time and can easily result in otherwise qualified buyers having to move on to a new property, leaving your home stuck on the market.

In these scenarios it is important to remember that the buyers are already borrowing a substantial sum so adding a comparable amount to the cost of the home can be a reasonable concession on both ends to make the sale a reality. However, it is important to remember that the total cost of the home must be reasonable based on the appraisal, otherwise the lender on the loan might not approve it.

Understand what draws buyers to houses

For most buyers, buying a new home isn't about getting the greatest possible value for their money, it is about making a real connection with a house as a place that could be home. As such, when you are selling, it is important to hold off on lists of facts and figures regarding amounts spent remodeling and maintaining and more about making the extra effort to show your home in the best light possible. Letting people talk themselves into making an offer without getting into the nitty gritty will keep you from appearing needy or over eager which will allow you to negotiate from a place of power instead.

Be aware of common tactics

There are a number of common types of negotiation tactics that buyers will try that can all be mitigated with the right response. The first common type of buyer is the sort who is always going to have to run any numbers past a third party before giving any type of concrete answer. It is important to not be fooled, however, as this is simply a way to try and cut down the final price a little more. Stop this strategy in its tracks by asking buyers if there is anyone they would like to be present in order to finalize the specifics. A similar tactic is the good cop/bad cop routine where the one party is extremely enthusiastic while the other is extremely negative. The solution here is the same, negotiate with all parties at once.

Another common buyer negotiation tactic is to try and get you to agree to a number of small concessions that ultimately add up to a surprising amount. To counter this strategy, take the time to precisely document everything that has been agreed to on both sides and refer to the document when additions are suggested. Remind them that an agreement is already in place and that changing anything now would result in a new offer having to be submitted. A variation on this technique is the buyer who instead blurts out an offer, usually quiet favorable to them, in an effort to shock you into agreeing.

Finally, buyers may ask what are known as trial balloon questions, which are questions that are designed to feel out the seller while not revealing any new information about the buyer. Trial balloon questions include things like how firm the list price is, or if you would be interested in financing the property without a lender. If you find yourself constantly bombarded with questions, retaliate with some of your own by asking what their response to your response might be.

Chapter 12: Negotiation Tips for Introverts

Negotiating for anything, much less important things like salaries and the price on major purchases likes cars and homes can be difficult for anyone, but for those with introvert personalities it can seem practically impossible. The first step to making the negotiation process possible, if not pleasurable, is to understand that there are plenty of people in the same boat and to know that this particular issue can be overcome with practice. The secret to being able to successfully negotiate as an introvert is to stop trying to act like an extrovert and to instead play to the strengths that being an introvert offers.

Have a clear goal

Make sure you take the time to visualize a clear goal before you start any negotiation. If you head into things by simply hoping for the best, it is likely that your natural tendencies will take over and things will go down a less productive path. Prior to entering into the negotiation it is important to research the topic thoroughly and understand your personal reasonable limits in advanced. Having a clear understanding of what lines can and cannot be crossed beforehand will make any actual negotiating much more manageable.

If it seems as though the person you are negotiating with is either unwilling or unable to help you reach your reasonable, and in all likelihood attainable goals, you must be willing to walk away. This isn't a rude behavior or one that will have negative consequences later on, no matter what your brain might tell you to the contrary, this is simply a thing that people do when negotiations don't go as planned. Stick to your guns and you will see positive results.

It helps to understand that you have value

When it comes to any negotiation, but especially those that involved trained sales people, the entire negotiation process can be made to seem much more manageable as long as you keep in mind the fact that the person you are dealing with ultimately wants your business. Negotiation doesn't have to be about conflict, in many situations you can still save yourself a substantial amount of money without sacrificing the other party's happiness. Don't let your imagine get carried away, the only thing that will happen if you try and fail to manage a successful negotiation is that the price of the goods or service in question will remain the same, there is no real downside when it comes to negotiating.

Use silence to your advantage

As an introvert it is likely that you are used to silence more than the average extrovert and negotiations are one of the rare times that you can use this fact to your advantage. When the person you are negotiating with says something that you don't agree with, silence is one of the most poignant ways to make this fact known. Don't be afraid to let the silence linger, state your piece and let them fill in the blanks with nervous chatter, doing so will leave you in a position of power for whatever comes next.

Know yourself

If you are like most introverts than being out amongst the populace is a draining experience from which you need to recharge in order to remain at your best. If this is true for you, then do yourself a favor and schedule negotiation sessions first thing in the morning so you are at your best when it comes to interacting with others. If this is not an option consider email negotiation, or possibly even something over the phone, to prevent the pitfalls of personal interaction. You will be surprised at just how much of a difference the right mindset will make when it comes to negotiating successfully.

The same is true when it comes to focusing on the task at hand. Don't worry about the other party, focus on your goals for the current negotiation and don't let interpersonal factors cloud your judgment. As long as you did the required research on the topic in question then your request is most likely perfectly reasonable which means you have every right to voice it with certainty. With that in mind, all you need to do is to choose a role that can best get you the things you are looking for. The person you are negotiating with doesn't know the real you which can provide you with the opportunity to act the way a person would who is looking to get the most out of the current scenario. Give yourself the freedom to try out different roles and you will be surprised at the results.

Take the right tone
Negotiation can be difficult for introverts because it can be difficult to determine the right level of friendliness as compared to aggressiveness. In most scenarios the best choice is to go with a mix of friendly yet forceful, aim for the tone that actors use in movies where they call someone friend, except it is clear that the two people are decidedly not friends. You want to make it clear that you are being reasonable while at the same time projecting the fact that you will not be pushed around.

If you find that type of tone difficult, consider the benefactors of the results, are you working to get a better price on a new car to ensure your kids can get to where they need to be on time? What about the future spouse and child that will share the new home with you if you can only afford it? Maybe you simply want a bigger yard for your dog to call home. Regardless, think about who you are really negotiating for and you will be surprised how much easier it is to take what is rightfully yours.

Practice, practice, practice
If you remain nervous about an upcoming attempt at negotiation, consider practicing with a friend or loved one beforehand to mitigate performance anxiety. Practicing vocalizing the things you want can go a long way towards making them easier to say when the time is right. This exercise can also help you to understand the back and forth flow that is part of many negotiations, practice until you are comfortable taking the time to think offers through rather than agreeing out of reflex. Take the time you need to make the decision that is best for you and don't forget to get everything that has been said in writing, just in case.

Chapter 13: Surprising Goods and Services You Can Negotiate For

While everyone knows to expect to haggle when it comes to common things like raises and buying a car, the best negotiators understand that when it comes to trying to get a better deal, nothing is off limits.

Cell phone and Internet contracts
Contrary to what the companies providing you with these services want you to believe, the amounts that you pay for them are actually quite flexible. If you take the time to call them up and make it seem as though you are interested in cancelling your service; you will be surprised at how willing the person on the other end of the phone is to suddenly make a deal. If the first person on the phone insists that there is nothing they can do, ask for the customer retention department. The company is interested in keeping you as a customer as opposed to trying to find someone off the street to replace you, make them work for it.

Furniture
When it comes to large items like mattresses and couches, the manufactures of these items tend to set a minimum that they can be sold at which companies can then adhere to or possibly mark them up from there. Stores that sell them at the existing prices will tell you so and those that don't will instead be willing to work with you in some capacity, either way, you win. Even if the price is non-negotiable, consider asking for additional benefits or items with your purchase, at the very least you should be able to get them to throw in free shipping even if it is not typically offered.

When it comes to finding places willing to negotiate, always look for family run stores as opposed to chains and don't underestimate the allure of paying in cash. In these scenarios it is important to always ask to speak with the owner directly. When doing so, keep in mind that furniture is often marked up as much as 75 percent over purchase price, remain firm and don't be afraid to leave your number and walk away. While it isn't a quick or easy way to purchase new furniture, it will work at least as often as not.

Medical Expenses
When it comes to medical expenses that are not covered by your insurance, hospitals and doctors' offices typically have systems in place to ensure they at least are able to get paid for some of what was originally owed. Medical expenses are the most commonly unpaid form of debt so many institutions are willing to work with you rather than take a potential loss. This doesn't mean they will do so willing, however, and you will need to persevere through what is likely going to be several layers of red tape before you reach someone who will make a concession. Remain firm in your assertions that you cannot in anyway pay the amount present and you will eventually begin to make headway.

Vacation days
When it comes to getting the most out of a new job, most people take the number of vacation days they are presented with for granted. However, in scenarios where the monetary budget is tight, asking for a few extra paid vacation days to balance things out is a surprisingly painless for everyone to get what they want out of the negotiation. To make the most out of this negotiation tactic it is important to research trends in similar jobs in your industry, once you find a few examples of perks outside of what you are being offered, consider how they compare to your complete package and if your new job comes up wanting consider how best to compare the two and make suggestions in regards to corrections.

Gym memberships

Gym memberships are another scenario where the prices are actually quite a bit more flexible than they initially might appear. For example, those who sign up or renew their memberships around the beginning of the year are likely to get better deals, the same goes for the end of the summer when gym memberships typically drop off as the desire to look good by the pool wears off for another year. If you aren't interested in waiting, instead consider doing research as to average membership prices and after getting a free trial membership, bring your findings to the person who is in charge of customer retention. Remain firm in your commitment to a better deal and you will be surprised what you can get away with.

Professional services

There is no law setting the cost for the services provided by professionals like lawyers and dentists. This means that there is nothing to stop them from offering you a better deal if you are simply willing to ask for it. Any time you are quoted a price, there is no reason not to try and make it a little bit more reasonable. Keep in mind that the worst thing that anyone is ever going to say is no and you will be surprised how malleable even the most set in stone prices really are.

Conclusion

Thank you again for choosing this book. Hopefully it has been able to provide you will all of the information you need to take your negotiation game to the next level. Remember, negotiation is a skill and like any other skill it requires practice to master properly. Find the time to practice negotiating minor matters with friends and strangers and use the time to learn to read body language and anticipate arguments on the fly. Over time you will find that complex tactics come to you unbidden when the need for them arises; and even better, you will have created a number of your own.

If you found this book useful in anyway and feel the need to leave a star rating or review, thank you, it is most appreciated.

Free membership into the Mastermind Self Development Group!

For a limited time, you can join the Mastermind Self Development Group for free! You will receive videos and articles from top authorities in self development as well as a special group only offers on new books and training programs. There will also be a monthly member only draw that gives you a chance to win any book from your Kindle wish list!

If you sign up through this link http://www.mastermindselfdevelopment.com/specialreport you will also get a special free report on the Wheel of Life. This report will give you a visual look at your current life and then take you through a series of exercises that will help you plan what your perfect life looks like. The workbook does not end there; we then take you through a process to help you plan how to achieve that perfect life. The process is very powerful and has the potential to change your life forever. Join the group now and start to change your life! http://www.mastermindselfdevelopment.com/specialreport

MASTERMIND
Self Development